Sea Mammals

Bottlenose Dolphin

Pygmy Right Whale

Dall's Porpoise

Sea Mammals

Whales, porpoises, and dolphins are sea mammals. Land mammals breathe with lungs. Sea mammals have lungs too. They can stay underwater for a long time. They must come to the surface to breathe. They breathe through a blowhole on top of their head.

Porpoises and dolphins are much smaller than the great whales, but they are the same in many ways. They all have sleek bodies for swimming. They have a layer of blubber under their skin to keep them warm in the cold ocean. They have flippers on their sides and tails called flukes. They give birth to live babies (calves). The babies feed on their mother's milk.

More Sea Mammals

Seal

Sea Lion

Sea Otter

Walrus

More Sea Mammals

Many sea mammals live near land. Sea lions, seals, and walruses come ashore part of the day to sunbathe. Otters spend almost all of their time in the water.

Sea lions, seals, and walruses have smooth skin and a layer of blubber. Otters do not have blubber. They have a very thick fur coat that helps keep them warm. They must also eat a lot of food for fuel to warm them.

Like other mammals, these sea mammals breathe air with lungs. They have live babies that are fed milk by their mothers.

Types of Whales

Toothed Whale

Bottlenosed Dolphin

Baleen Whale

Minke Whale

Types of Whales

There are two different groups of whales—those that have teeth and those that do not.

Toothed whales are hunters. They work harder for a meal than the baleen whales. Sometimes toothed whales work together in groups to surround and kill their prey. They eat fish and other sea mammals. Toothed whales are usually smaller than the baleen whales.

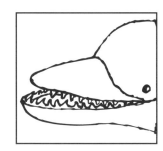

Baleen whales strain small animals called **plankton** out of the water. Baleen is made from the same material as fins and tails. The baleen hangs down from the whale's top jaw. The whale gulps in water. The water is pushed out through the baleen. The plankton stays in the whale's mouth and is swallowed.

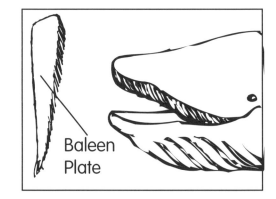

Baleen Plate

Whale Life Cycle

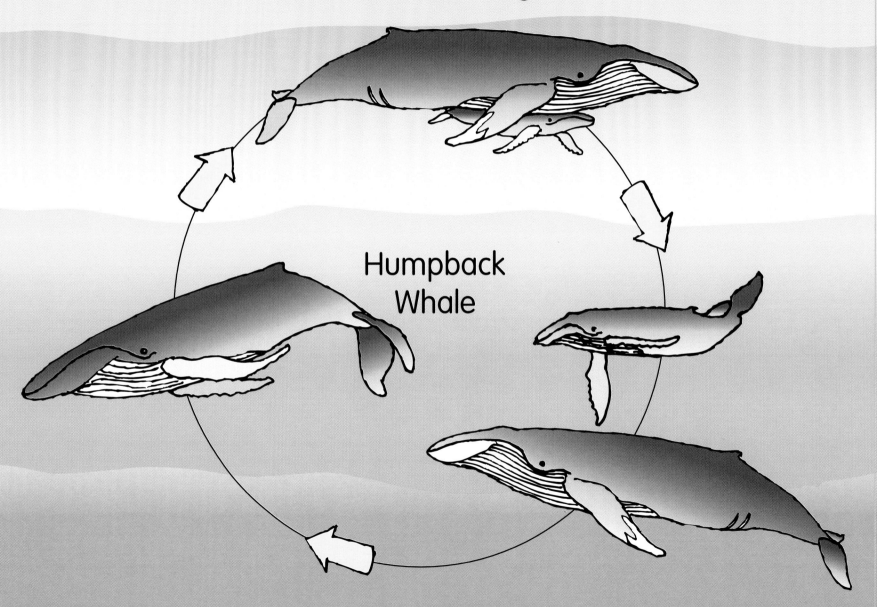

Humpback Whale

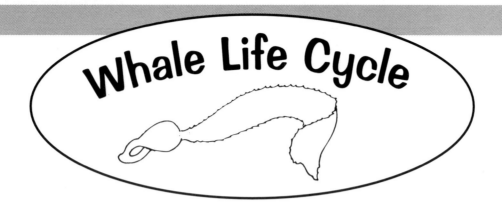

Whale Life Cycle

A mother whale gives birth to one calf. When it is born, she must help it get to the surface to get its first breath of air. Mother whales take good care of their calves.

Whale calves look like adult whales, only smaller. Some kinds of baby whales drink as much as 130 gallons (490 liters) of milk a day. They grow quickly on the rich milk fed them by their mothers. A blue whale calf gains over 8 pounds (3.5 kilograms) an hour for many months.

The growing calf has a lot to learn. As it grows, it practices diving, holding its breath, and getting food. After many months it is able to care for itself.

Whale and Fish

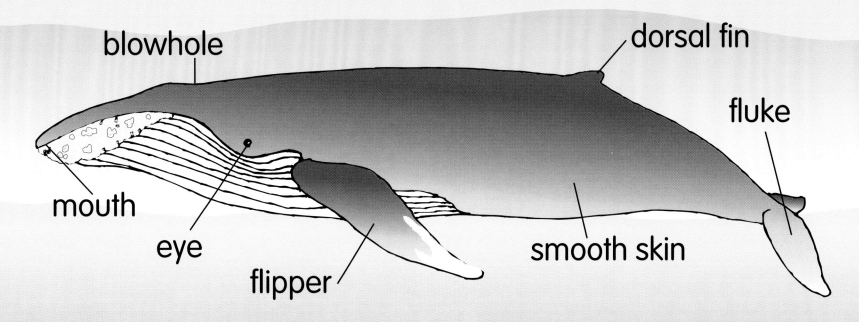

blowhole

dorsal fin

fluke

mouth

eye

smooth skin

flipper

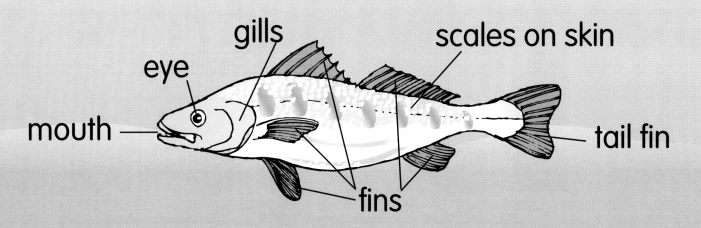

gills

scales on skin

eye

mouth

fins

tail fin

Whale and Fish

They both live in the ocean, but a fish and a whale are different in many ways.

A whale:
- has smooth skin
- inhales through a blowhole
- breathes with lungs
- gives birth to live babies and feeds them milk
- swims by moving its tail up and down

A fish:
- has skin covered in scales
- takes water in through its mouth
- has gills to take oxygen from the water
- has babies that hatch from eggs
- swims by moving its tail from side to side

Fish with Bone Skeletons

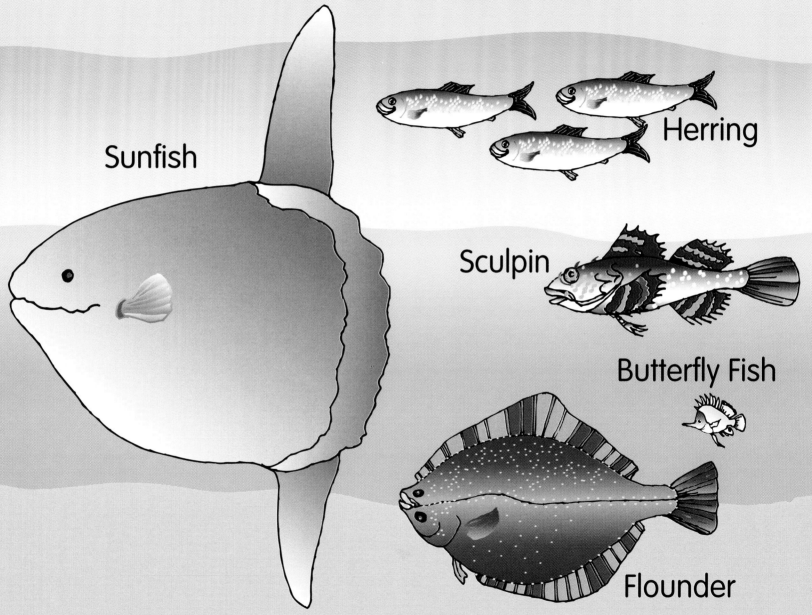

Sunfish

Herring

Sculpin

Butterfly Fish

Flounder

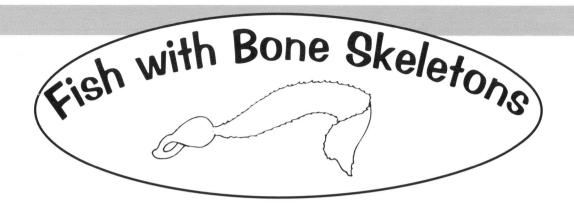

Fish with Bone Skeletons

The fish on this card are different in color, shape, and size. But they are alike in these ways:

- They have skeletons of bone.
- They get their oxygen from the water using gills.
- They swim using fins.
- They have scales.
- Most have swimbladders. Swimbladders are used to help fish stay in one place without using a lot of energy.
- They are cold-blooded. This means their bodies are the same temperature as the water around them. If it is cold, the fish are cold. If it is hot, the fish are hot.

Different kinds of fish live in different parts of the ocean. Herring and sunfish live in the open ocean. Flounder and sculpins live on the bottom of the sea. Butterfly fish live in a coral reef.

Fish with Skeletons of Cartilage

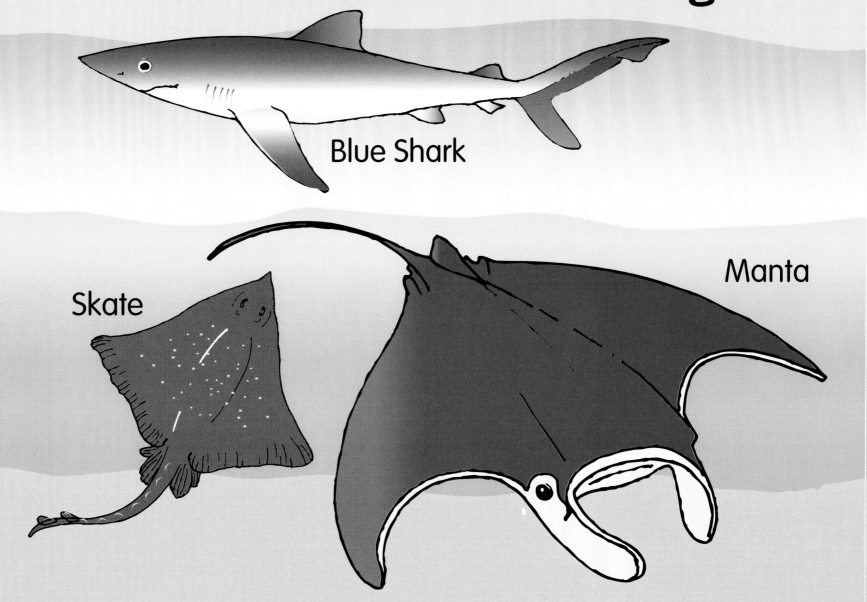

Blue Shark

Skate

Manta

Fish with Skeletons of Cartilage

These fish all have skeletons made of flexible **cartilage** (**kar** tuh lij). Cartilage is very strong, but it bends easier than bone. These fish have gill slits for breathing. They do not have swim bladders, so they must keep moving to keep from sinking.

Most sharks have long, sleek bodies. They usually have five gill slits. Sharks have rough skin covered in tiny teeth (**denticles**). Most sharks hunt for fish or small sea mammals to eat. A few kinds of sharks eat shellfish off the bottom of the sea. The largest shark is the whale shark. It eats plankton and small fish that it sifts out of the sea.

Skates and rays are very flat with fins like large wings. Rays have long whip-like tails with poison stingers. Skates and rays stay buried in sand during the day. They come out at night to feed on small animals with shells.

Unusual Fish

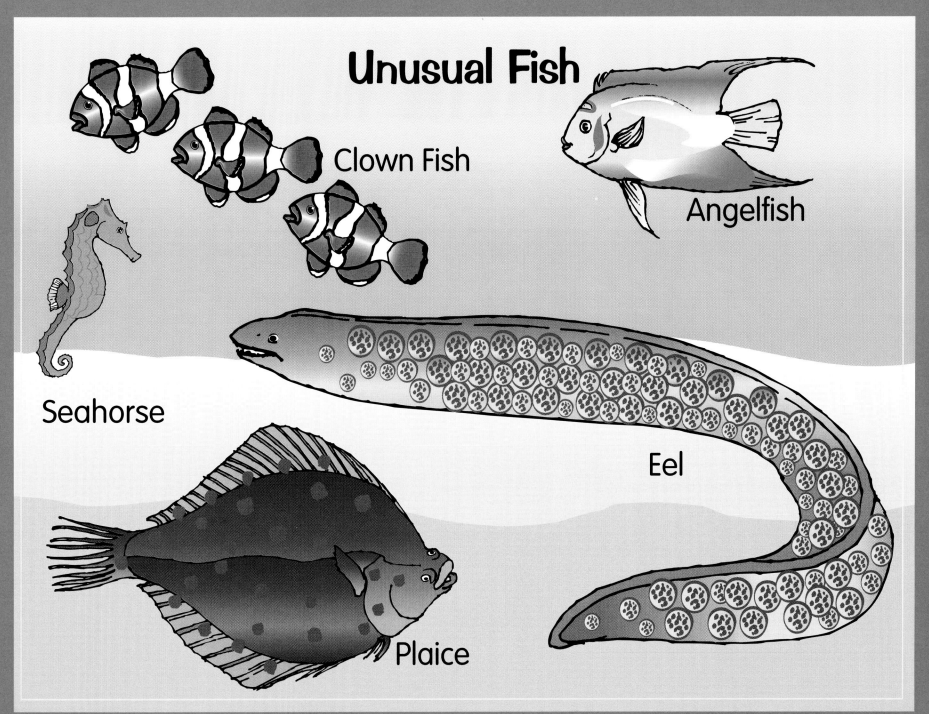

Clown Fish

Angelfish

Seahorse

Eel

Plaice

Unusual Fish

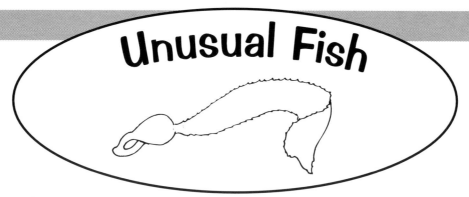

Oceans are filled with unusual fish. Some have beautiful colors and designs. Others are strange looking. Some don't look like fish at all.

Eels look more like snakes than fish. They wiggle their long bodies through the water. They have narrow fins along their backs. Their skin is smooth and slippery.

Tiny seahorses swim with their heads up and tails down. They swim by wiggling their back fin. Seahorses can change colors. This helps them hide in sea grasses or coral. Male seahorses carry the eggs in pouches until the babies hatch.

Plaice are a kind of flatfish that live on the bottom of the sea bed. Their bodies are thin and flat. Both of their eyes are on the same side of their heads. Flatfish bury themselves in sand or gravel with just their eyes showing.

Some fish use dots, stripes, or splashes of color to help them hide. Lying still among ocean plants, they look like spots of light and shadows rather than fish.

How Fish Are Born

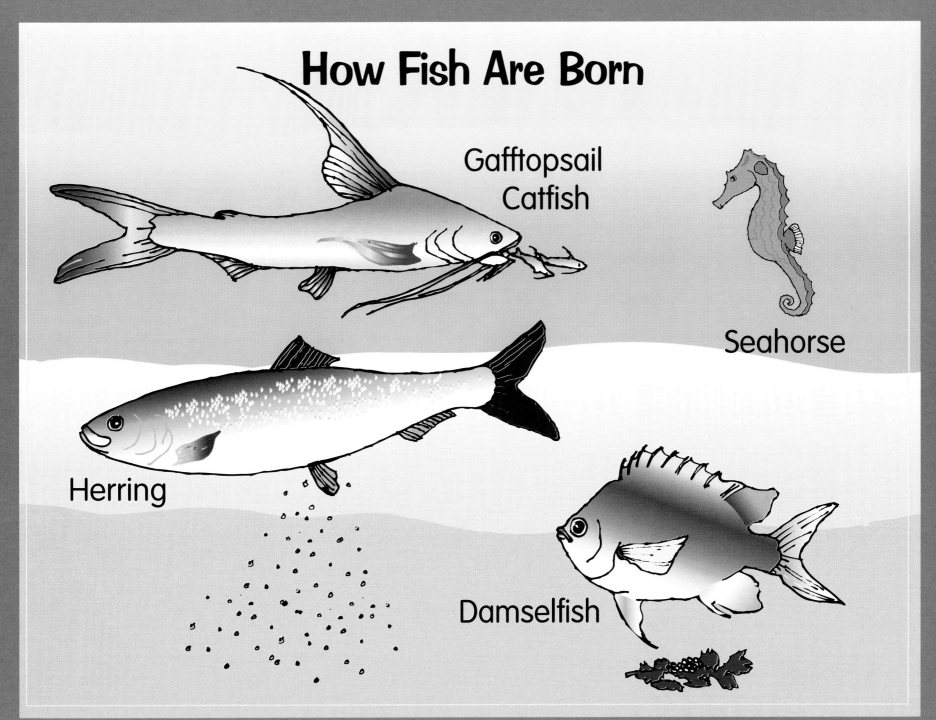

Gafftopsail
Catfish

Seahorse

Herring

Damselfish

How Fish Are Born

Most fish just lay their eggs in the water. Then the parent swims away. Some of the eggs grow and hatch, but many are eaten by other fish. When they hatch, the baby fish have to take care of themselves. Some are eaten by other fish. Some grow up to lay their own eggs.

Some parents take care of their eggs.

Nest builders scoop out a nest in the rocks or sandy sea bottom and lay their eggs in the nest. The eggs are covered with pebbles or sand. Then the parent swims away.

Some fish have live babies. The babies grow inside the mother until they are big enough to be born.

Other fish carry the eggs in different ways. Seahorse females lay their eggs in a pouch on the male seahorse. He carries the eggs until they hatch. There is even a fish that carries the eggs in its mouth until they hatch. Then the babies swim out of the mother's mouth.

Swell Shark Life Cycle

egg
case

pup

Swell Shark Life Cycle

A swell shark lays its egg case on the ocean floor. You can see the head and tail of the baby swell shark beginning to form.

The baby begins to have the shape, color, and markings of an adult swell shark.

When a swell shark pup hatches from its egg case, it looks like the adult, only much smaller. It will continue to grow until it is as large as its parents.

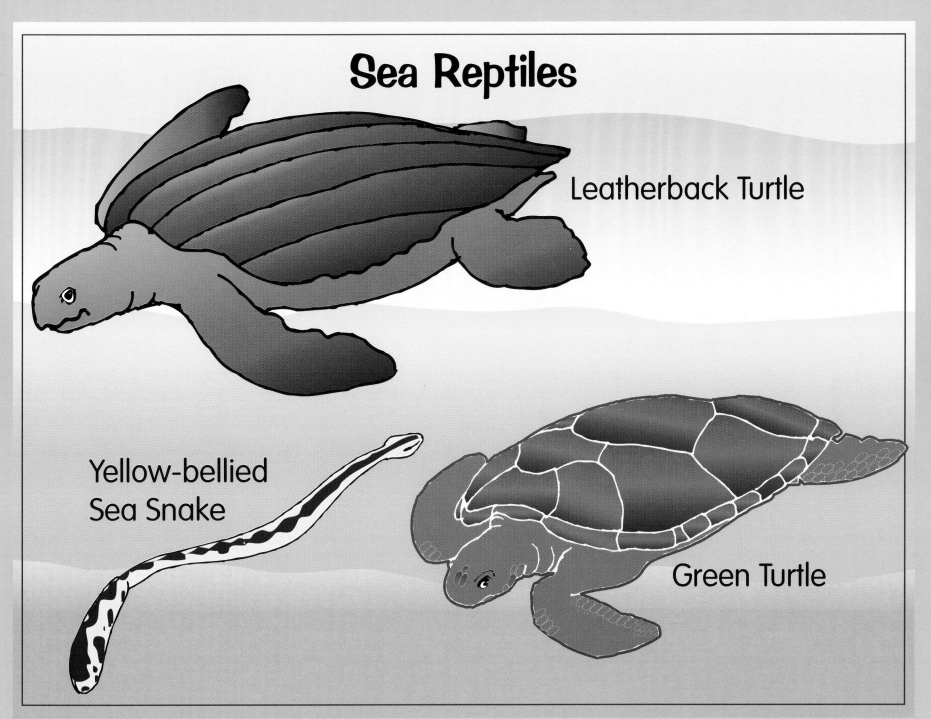

Sea Reptiles

Leatherback Turtle

Yellow-bellied
Sea Snake

Green Turtle

Sea Reptiles

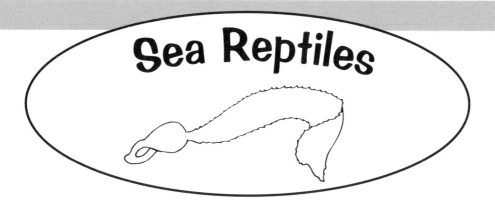

Sea turtles and sea snakes are reptiles. Most of their life is spent in water. They have lungs so they must come to the surface to breathe. Both sea snakes and sea turtles can stay underwater for a long time.

Sea snakes live in the warm tropical seas. They have flattened tails that they use like paddles while swimming. Most sea snakes have live young in the water. The baby snakes can swim as soon as they are born. Sea snakes use poison to kill the fish they eat.

Sea turtles live around the world in warm seas. They have flippers for swimming and strong jaws to crush the shells of sea animals they eat. Sea turtles come on land to lay their eggs. The female digs a hole in the sand and lays as many as 100 eggs. She covers up the eggs and returns to the sea. When the eggs hatch, the young turtles crawl to the water and swim away.

Sea Turtle Life Cycle

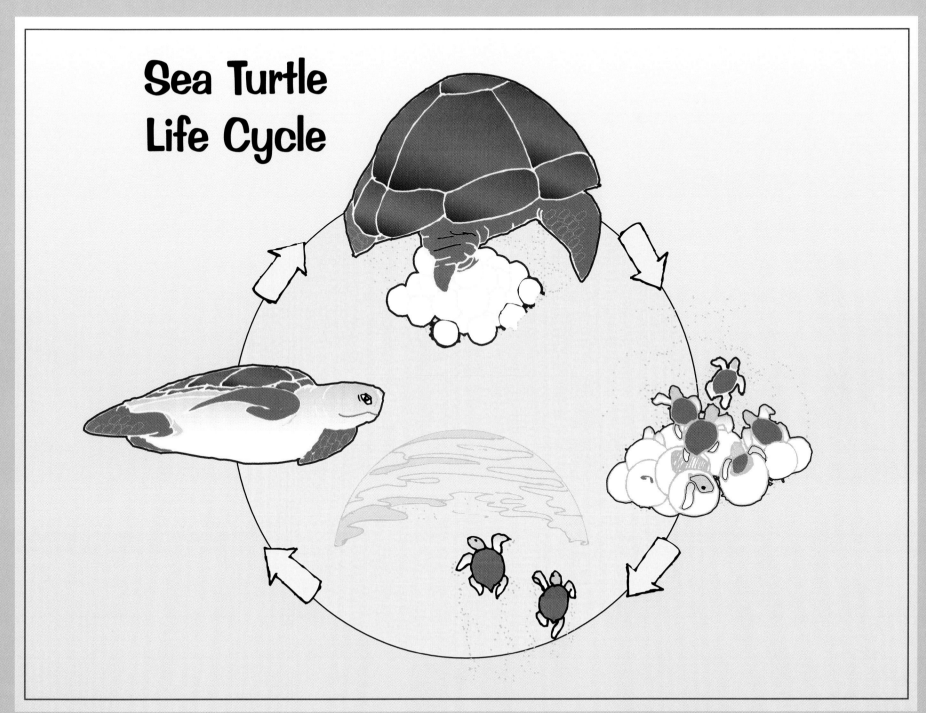

Sea Turtle Life Cycle

The female sea turtle digs a hole in the sand. She lays up to 100 eggs in the hole. She covers up the hole and crawls back to the sea. She never returns to the nest.

When the eggs hatch, the tiny turtles crawl out of the shells. They must dig their way to the surface of the sand.

The tiny turtles crawl across the beach to the water. They are ready to swim and to find food.

Each year the turtles grow larger until they are adults.

Sea Birds

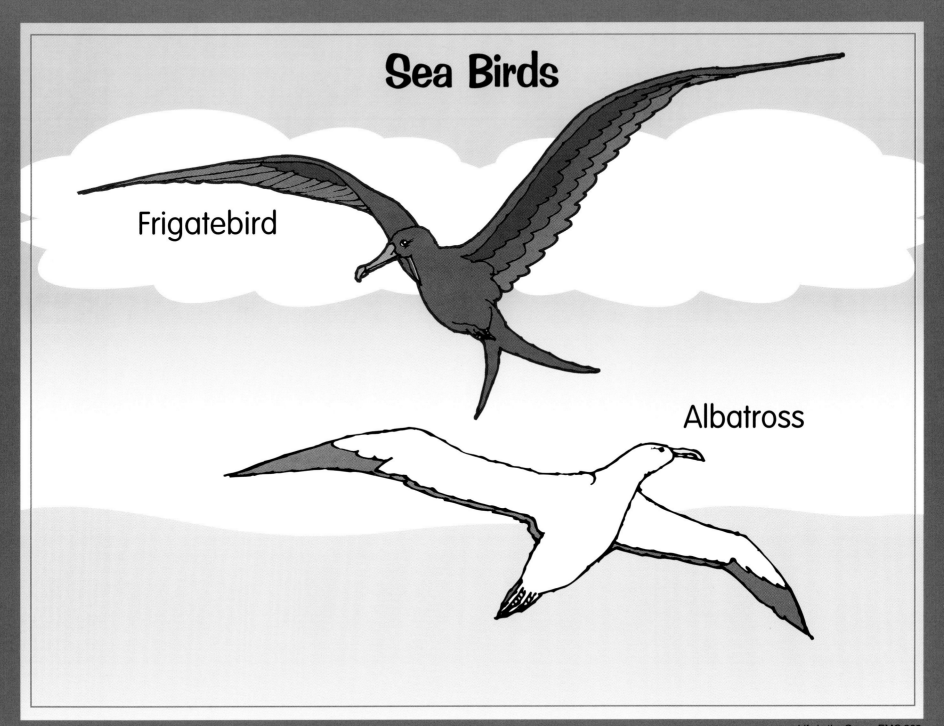

Frigatebird

Albatross

Sea Birds

Sea birds are birds that get their food from the sea. Some seabirds spend almost all of their time soaring over the open seas. They may stay at sea for many months at a time. They land on the water to rest. They only come ashore to raise their young. The bodies of sea birds such as the albatross and frigate are built for long-distance flying. They have large wings and small, light bodies. They catch fish, shrimp, squid, and jellyfish as they swoop across the surface of the water.

An albatross is the largest of the sea birds. It soars on wind currents with its long, narrow wings.

Frigates can eat and sleep while flying. They spend so much time in the air, their legs and feet are not very good for walking. They are graceful in the air, but clumsy on land.

Diving Sea Birds

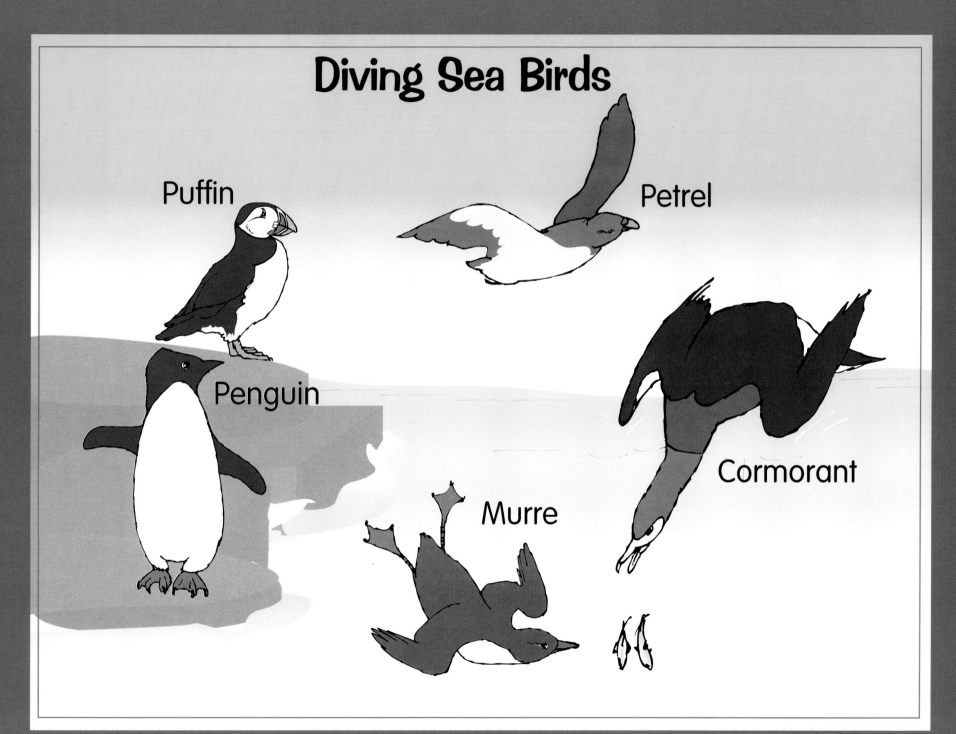

Puffin

Petrel

Penguin

Murre

Cormorant

Diving Sea Birds

Some sea birds are at home both flying and in the water. These diving sea birds have legs set toward the back of their bodies to help them move quickly and steer better when they dive. They are strong swimmers.

Diving sea birds have waterproof feathers. They spread oil on their feathers (**preen**) using their beaks. The oily feathers and a layer of fat help keep the birds warm and dry.

Diving sea birds live in colonies on shore where they lay their eggs. This is safer for the eggs and for the young birds.

Penguins can't fly at all, but they are great swimmers. They have sleek bodies for speed. They have short, stiff wings that they use as paddles.

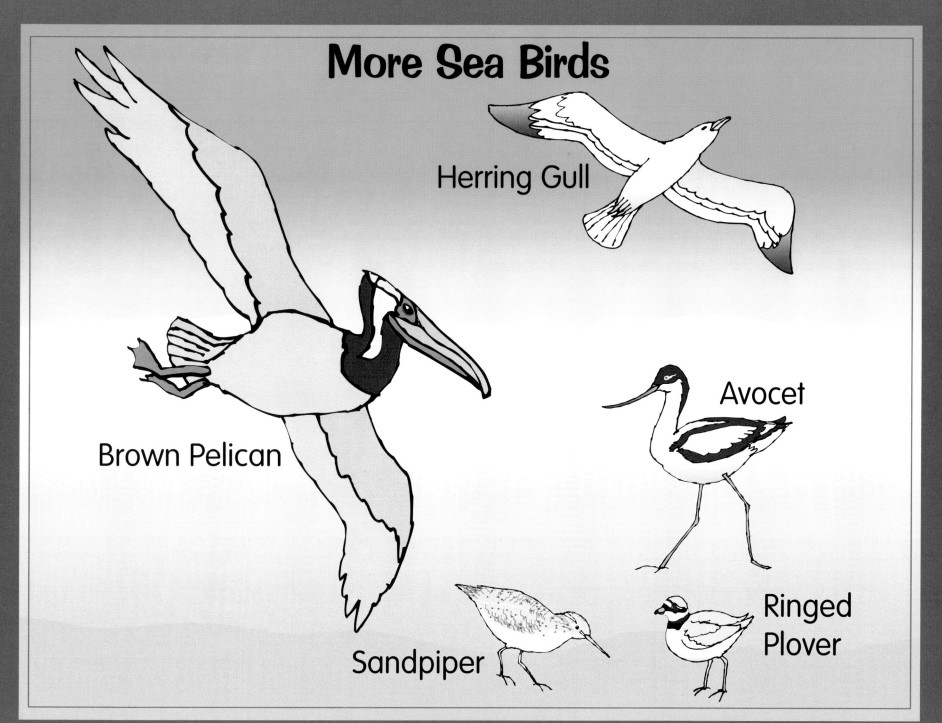

More Sea Birds

Herring Gull

Avocet

Brown Pelican

Sandpiper

Ringed
Plover

More Sea Birds

Along the shore you will see both flying birds and wading birds.

A flock of pelicans may fly by. They dive down below the surface of the water when they see fish. They scoop up water and fish in a pouch-like bill.

Gulls paddle on the water surface with webbed feet. They don't dive very often. Most gulls are scavengers and will eat anything they can find. Herring gulls also like crabs, clams, and other small sea animals. They will fly up into the sky with a clam and drop it onto rocks to break the shell open.

Wading birds such as the avocet and sandpiper have long legs for wading in the water. They have long bills for picking up food from tide pools and from water lapping up along the shore.

Herring Gull Life Cycle

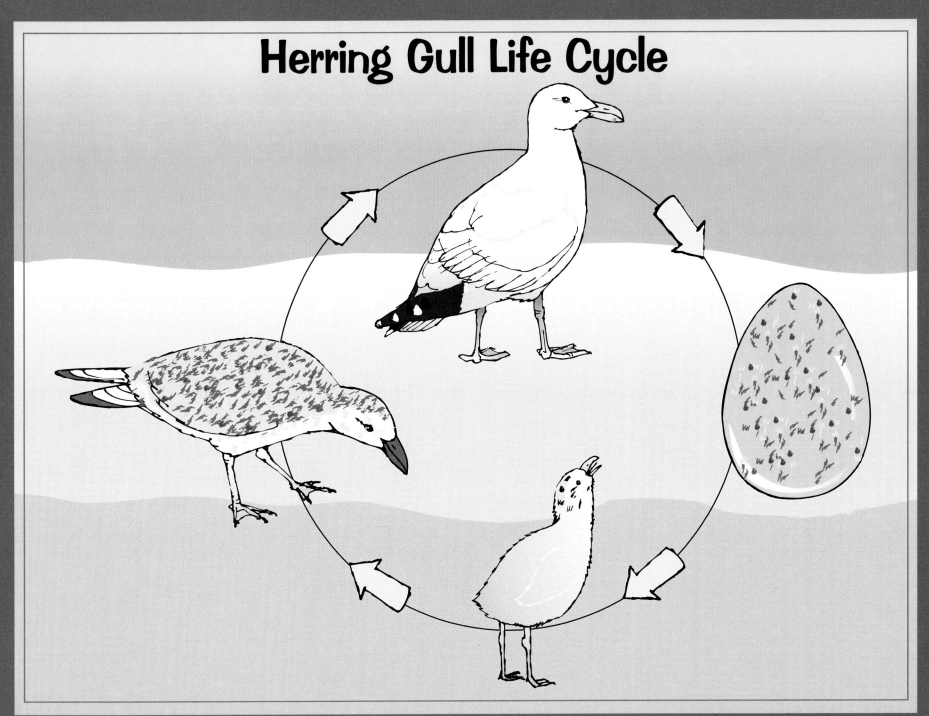

Herring Gull Life Cycle

The female herring gull builds a nest of sticks, seaweed, and other plants. She lays spotted eggs in the nest.

The chicks are wet when they hatch. Soon the feathers will dry and the fluffy, spotted chicks will be able to run around.

The chicks peck at a red spot on the adult's bill. This means "Feed me!" The adult coughs up food for the chicks to eat.

Young gulls are speckled with brown. They won't get their adult colors for a long time.

Adult herring gulls have white heads and tails. They have gray feathers on their wings and backs.

Mollusks with Shells

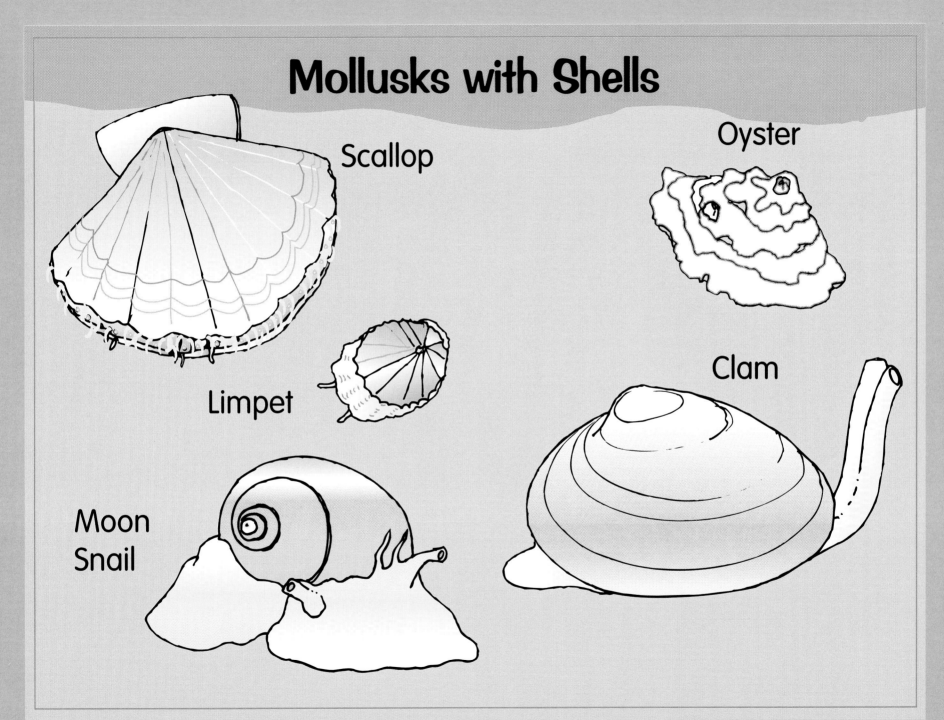

Scallop

Oyster

Limpet

Clam

Moon
Snail

Mollusks with Shells

All of these sea animals are **mollusks**. Mollusks have soft bodies with no bones. Some have shells on the outside. Some have a shell that grows inside. And some have no shell at all.

Scallops, clams, and oysters have two shells with soft bodies inside. When they open up their shells, water flows over their gills. The gills take oxygen and small bits of food from the water. The shell is closed tight for protection.

Limpets and moon snails are two kinds of sea snails that have one shell. They move on one muscular foot. They have tentacles for seeing and tentacles for feeling. A rough tongue scrapes, tears, and grinds food for the snails to eat.

Mollusks without Shells

Octopus

Squid

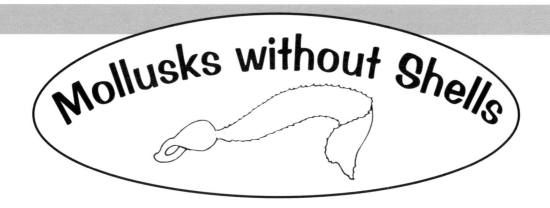

Mollusks without Shells

Octopuses and squid are **mollusks**. An octopus is a mollusk with no shell. A squid is a mollusk with a small piece of cartilage inside its body.

Both octopuses and squid have beaks and rough tongues for eating shrimp, crab, and fish. Both can change color to hide. They can give off a cloud of ink to escape danger. They swim by spurting jets of water.

An octopus has eight arms with suckers that help it hang onto rocks and to catch food. A squid has eight arms and two long tentacles.

Crustaceans

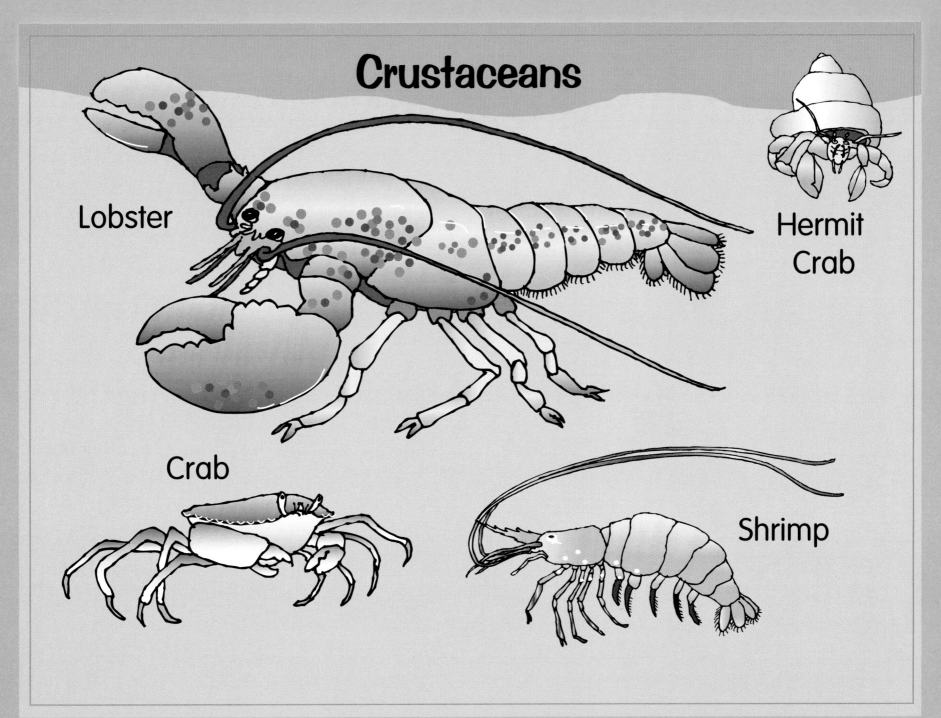

Lobster

Hermit Crab

Crab

Shrimp

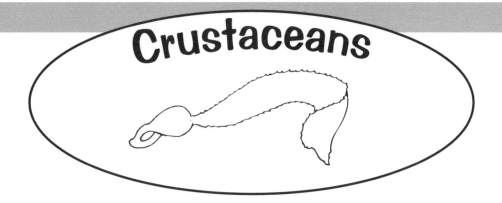

Crustaceans

Lobsters and crabs have a hard outside covering. They have two pairs of **antennae** (an **ten** ee) and ten legs. The front two legs have sharp claws called **pincers**. They use these claws to crush their food. They breathe with gills. Some lobsters and crabs can stay on land for a long time.

A lobster has a long body divided into parts. A crab has a wide, one-piece body.

When lobsters, crabs, and prawns grow bigger, they crawl out of their old shells and grow new, bigger ones.

The little hermit crab doesn't have a hard shell. It finds an empty shell left by a sea snail and crawls in. When it becomes too big for the shell, it moves out and finds a bigger one.

More Invertebrates

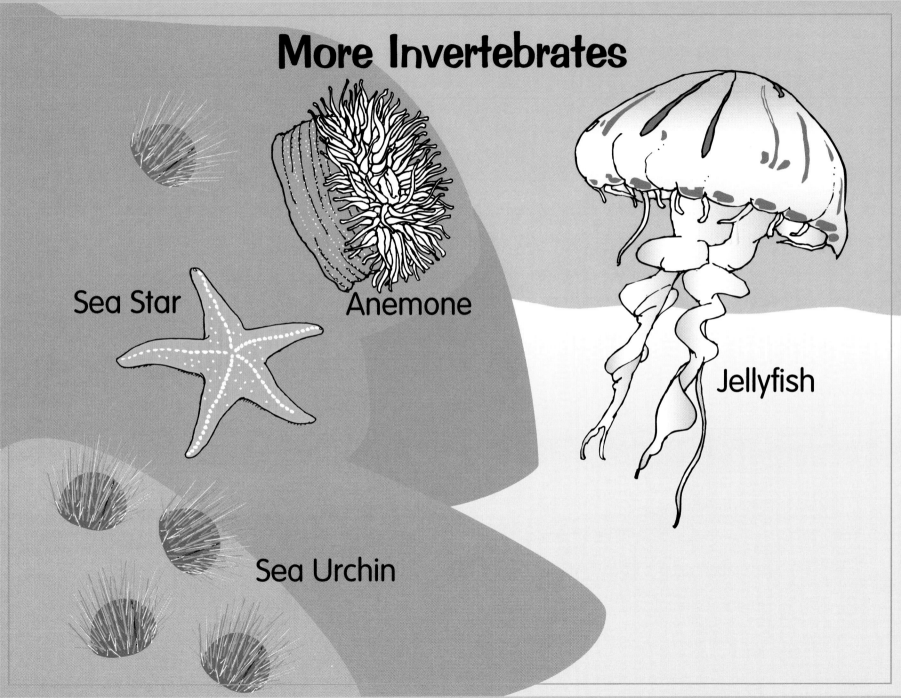

Sea Star

Anemone

Jellyfish

Sea Urchin

More Invertebrates

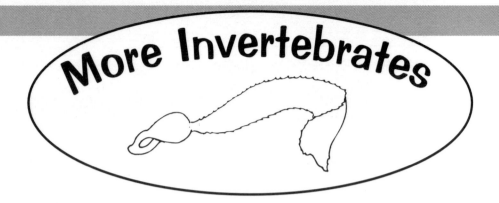

A sea star (starfish) has five or more rays sticking out from the center of its body. It moves on tiny tube feet that act like suction cups. It uses its rays to pull open shellfish. A sea star puts its stomach into the shell of the animal it wants to eat. When it is finished eating, the sea star pulls its stomach back inside its body.

A sea urchin has long spines all over its body. It looks like a pincushion. It uses its spines to move it from place to place. Most sea urchins eat by scraping seaweed from rocks.

A sea anemone (uh **nem** uh nee) looks more like a flower attached to a rock than an animal. It is like a little bag with an opening on the top. Tentacles surround the top of its body. Stinging cells on the tentacles stun its prey. Then the tentacles pull the prey into the stomach in the center of the anemone.

A jellyfish is not a fish at all. It has a body shaped like a bell with a long mouth-tube hanging in the center. Tentacles (**ten** tuh kulz) with stinging cells surround the bell. It uses the stinging cells hanging down around its mouth to stun its prey.

Seaweed

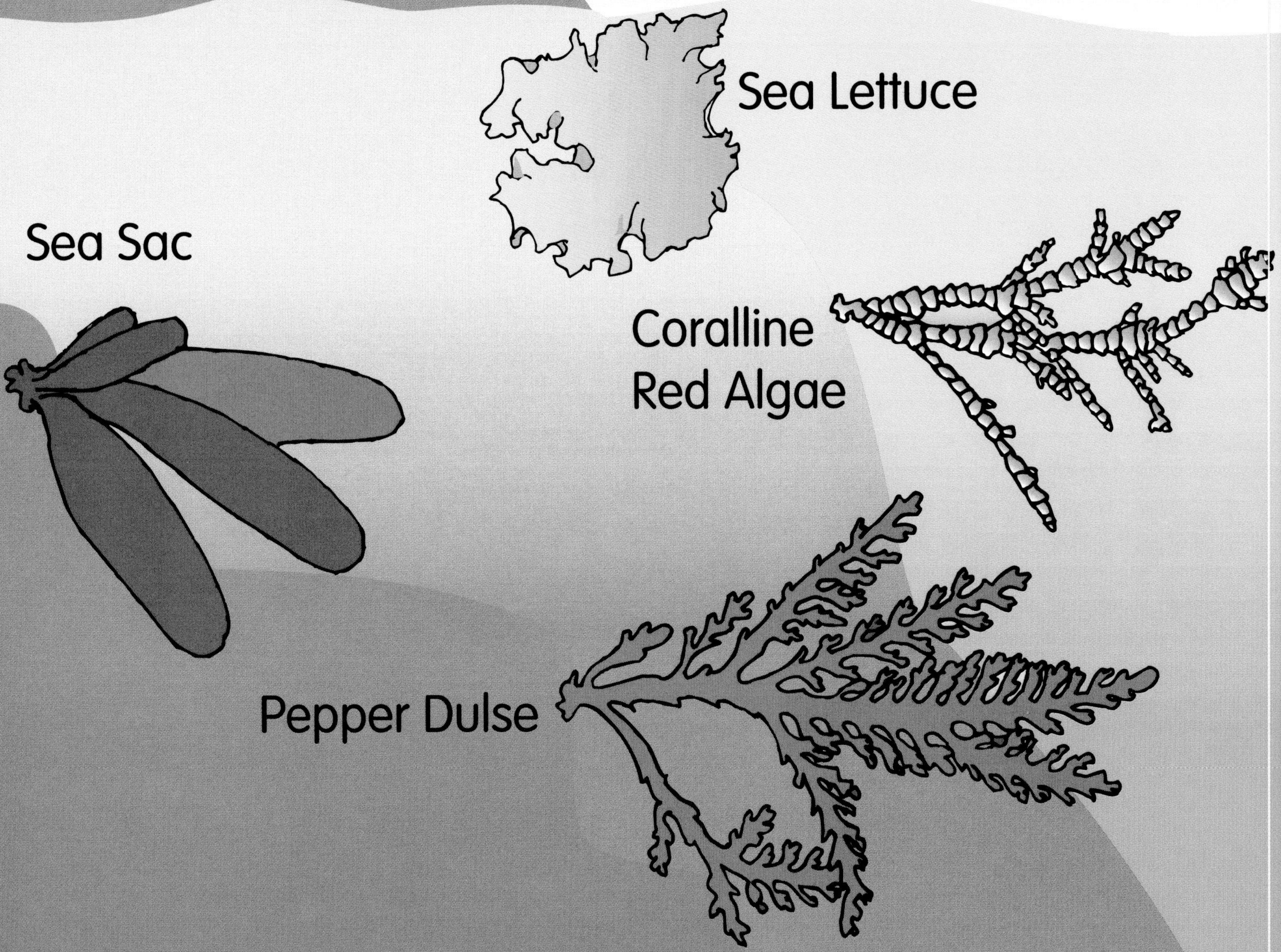

Sea Lettuce

Sea Sac

Coralline
Red Algae

Pepper Dulse

Seaweed

These seaweeds (**algae**) live in the shallow water along rocky seashores. They bend back and forth as waves move in and out. They can live out of the water until the next tide comes in. Many animals in tide pools eat the seaweeds.

Some seaweeds grow on other plants. Some grow on the shells of sea animals.

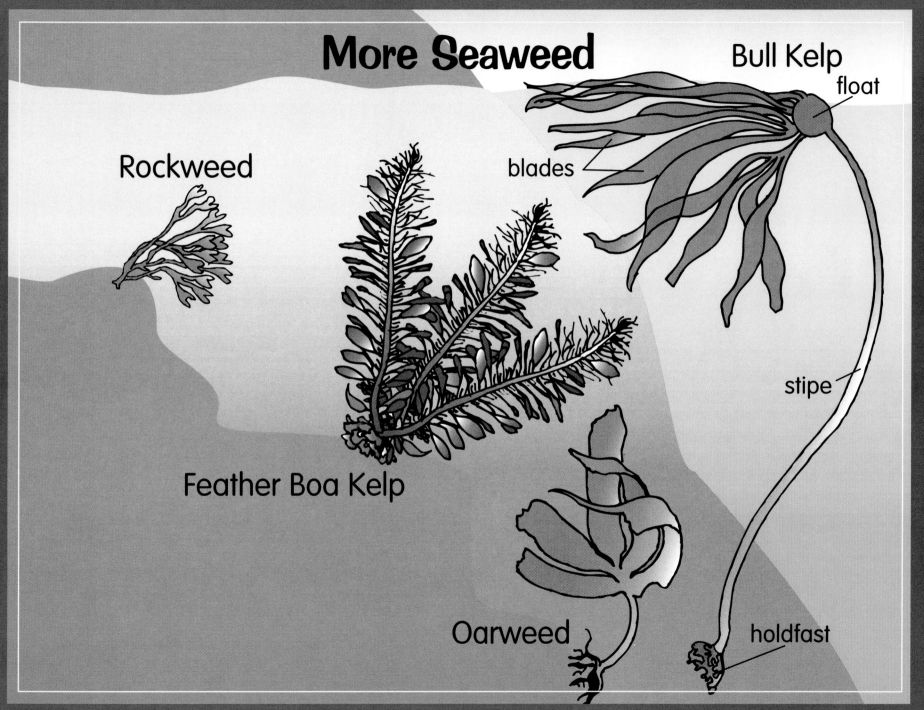

More Seaweed

Bull Kelp

float

blades

Rockweed

stipe

Feather Boa Kelp

Oarweed

holdfast

More Seaweed

These brown seaweeds (**algae**) grow along the coast. They need a hard surface to grow on. They do not have roots or leaves like land plants. They do have parts that anchor them to rocks or the ocean floor (**holdfasts**). They have parts that reach up to the surface to the sunlight (**stipe and blades**).

Giant Kelp

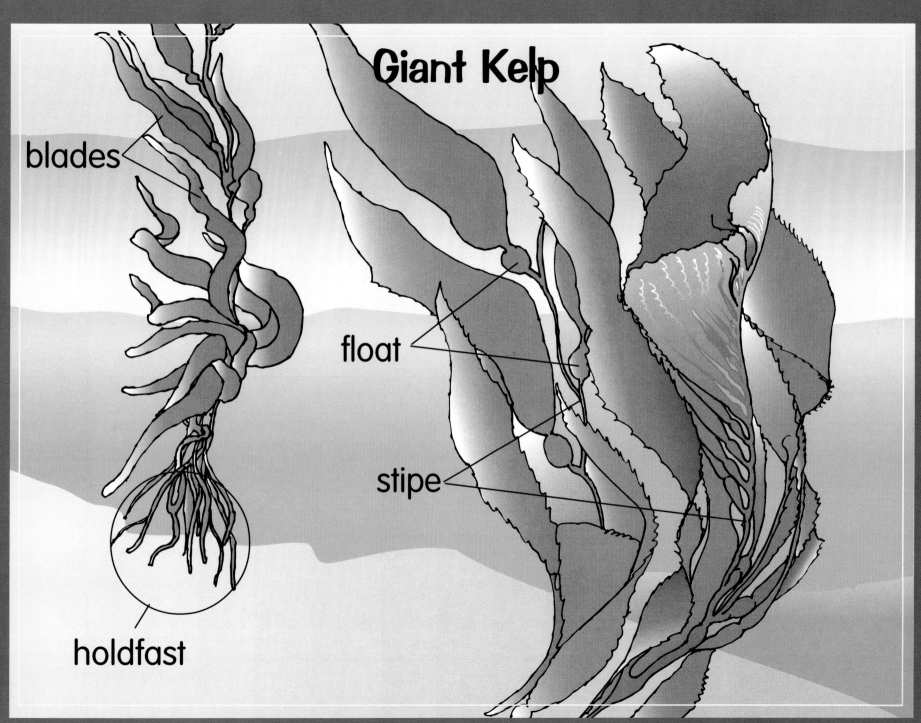

blades

float

stipe

holdfast

Giant Kelp

Giant kelp is the largest kind of brown seaweed (**algae**). It grows like a forest in the ocean. Some giant kelp can grow to be over 100 feet (34.8 meters) tall.

Each part of the kelp has a special job.

The **holdfast** looks like a root, but it is not a root. It just holds the kelp to a rock so it isn't swept away by the tide.

The **stipe** is like a stem. It is tough but bends without breaking as the water moves. The stipe carries food from the blades to the holdfast. **Floats**, bumps filled with air, help the blades float up to the surface of the water.

The **blades** look like leaves. They make the food for the plant. The blades also make **spores** that grow into new plants.

An Ocean Food Chain

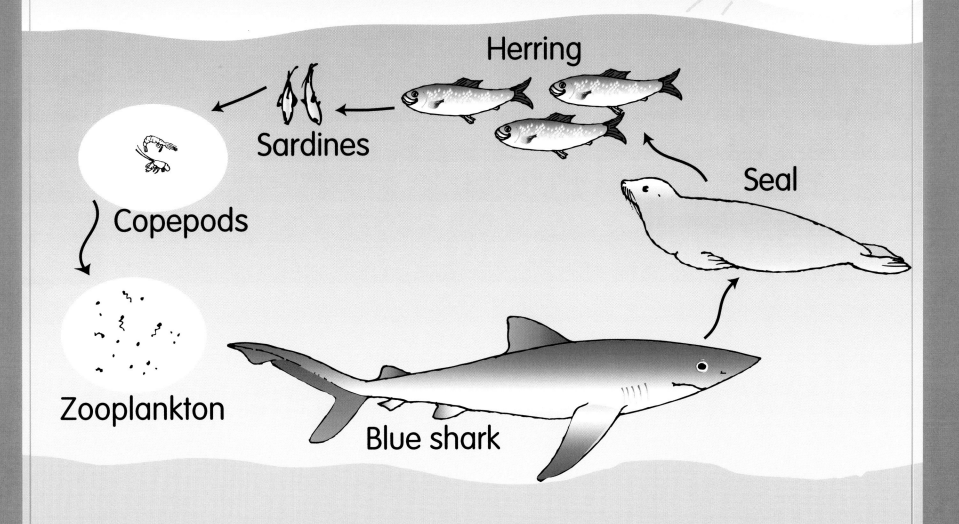

An Ocean Food Chain

Living things depend on each other for food and energy. This is true both in the ocean and on land. The way plants and animals eat each other is called a **food chain**. When several food chains are combined, it makes a **food web**.

You are a part of many ocean food webs. Fish and other sea animals are eaten by people. Seaweed is used in many of the foods we eat.